POWER & CONFLICT

AN AQA ESSAY WRITING GUIDE (9-1)

R. P. DAVIS

Copyright © 2020 Accolade Tuition Ltd
Published by Accolade Tuition Ltd
71-75 Shelton Street
Covent Garden
London WC2H 9JQ
www.accoladetuition.com
info@accoladetuition.com

ISBN 978-1-9163735-2-5

FIRST EDITION
1 3 5 7 9 10 8 6 4 2

For Norma.

CONTENTS

FOREWORD

In your GCSE English Literature exam, you will be presented with a single poem from the *Power and Conflict* anthology and a question that invites you to compare and contrast this poem with one other anthology poem of your choosing. Of course, there are many methods one *might* use to tackle this style of question. However, there is one particular technique which, due to its sophistication, most readily allows students to unlock the highest marks: namely, **the thematic method**.

To be clear, this study guide is *not* intended to walk you through the poems line-by-line: there are many great guides out there that do just that. No, this guide, by sifting through a series of mock exam questions, will demonstrate *how* to organise a response thematically and thus write a stellar essay: a skill we believe no other study guide adequately covers!

I have encountered students who have structured their essays all sorts of ways: some by writing about one or both of the poems line-by-line, others by identifying various language techniques and giving each its own paragraph. The method I'm advocating, on the other hand, involves picking out three themes that will allow you to holistically answer the question: these three themes will become the three content paragraphs of your essay, cushioned between a brief introduction and conclusion. Ideally, these themes will follow from one to the next to create a flowing argument. Within each of these thematic paragraphs, you can then ensure you are jumping through the mark scheme's hoops.

So to break things down further, each thematic paragraph will include various point-scoring components. In each paragraph, you will quote from the poem the exam board has set, offer analyses of these quotes, then discuss how the specific language techniques you have identified illustrate the theme you're discussing. In each paragraph, you will then quote from the second poem (the one you've chosen to write on), and, while analysing these quotes and remarking on language techniques, also explain not only how the second poem relates to the chosen theme, but also how it does so differently (or not!) from the first poem.

Don't worry if this all feels daunt-
ing. Throughout this guide, I will
be illustrating in great detail – by
means of examples – how to build
an essay of this kind.

The Irish coast. This is
likely the sort of cliff-face
Heaney was envisaging in
'Storm on the Island.'

The beauty of the thematic
approach is that, once you have
your themes, you suddenly have a
direction and a trajectory, and this
makes essay writing a whole lot easier. However, it must also be noted that extracting themes in the first place is something students often find tricky. I have come across many candidates who understand the poems inside out; but when they are

presented with a question under exam conditions, and the pressure kicks in, they find it tough to break their response down into themes. The fact of the matter is: the process is a *creative* one and the best themes require a bit of imagination.

In this guide, I shall take nine different exam-style questions, and put together nine essay plans that ensure that every poem in the anthology is discussed in depth at least once. These essay plans will also be accompanied by notes illustrating how we will be satisfying the mark scheme's criteria. Please do keep in mind that, when operating under timed conditions, your plans will necessarily be less detailed than those that appear in this volume.

A photo of World War One soldiers, taken in Merville, France. Two of the anthology's poems – Wlfred Owen's 'Exposure' & Ted Hughes's 'Bayonet Charge' – deal with the First World War.

Before I move forward in earnest, I believe it to be worthwhile to run through the four Assessment Objectives the exam board want you to cover in your response – if only to demonstrate how effective the thematic response can be. I would argue that the first Assessment Objective (AO1) – the one that wants candidates to 'read, understand and respond to texts' and which is worth 12 of the total 30 marks up for grabs – will be wholly satisfied by selecting strong themes, then fleshing them out with quotes. Indeed, when it comes to identifying the top-scoring candidates for AO1, the mark scheme explicitly tells examiners to look for a 'critical, exploratory, conceptualised response' that makes 'judicious use of precise references' – the word 'concept' is a synonym of theme, and 'judicious references' simply refers to quotes that appropriately support the theme you've chosen.

The second Assessment Objective (AO2) – which is also responsible for 12 marks – asks students to 'analyse the language, form and structure used by a writer to create meanings and effects, using relevant subject terminology where appropriate.' As noted, you will already be quoting from the poems as you back up your themes, and it is a natural progression to then analyse the language techniques used. In fact, this is far more effective than simply observing language techniques (personification here, alliteration there), because by discussing how the language techniques relates to and shapes the theme, you will also be demonstrating how the writer 'create[s] meanings and effects.'

Now, in my experience, language analysis is the most important element of AO2 – perhaps 8 of the 12 marks will go towards language analysis. You will also notice, however, that AO2 asks students to comment on 'form and structure.' Again, the thematic approach has your back – because though simply shoehorning in a point on form or structure will feel jarring, when you bring these points up while discussing a theme, as a means to further a thematic argument, you will again organically be discussing the way it 'create[s] meanings and effects.'

AO3 requires you to 'show understanding of the relationships between texts and the contexts in which they were written' and is responsible for a more modest 6 marks in total. These are easy enough to weave into a thematic argument; indeed, the theme gives the student a chance to bring up context in a relevant and fitting way. After all, you don't want it to look like you've just shoehorned a contextual factoid into the mix.

Finally, you have AO4 – known also as "spelling and grammar." Technically speaking, there are no AO4 marks up for grabs in this particular section of the paper. That said, I would still suggest that you take care on this front. The examiners are human beings, and if you are demonstrating a strong grasp of spelling and grammar, most examiners (whether rightly or wrongly!) will still be more inclined to mark your paper more generously.

My hope is that this book, by demonstrating how to tease out themes from a pair of poems, will help you feel more confident in doing so yourself. I believe it is also worth mentioning that the themes I have picked out are by no means definitive. Asked the very same question, someone else may pick out different themes, and write an answer that is just as good (if not better!). Obviously the exam is not likely to be fun – my memory of them is pretty much the exact opposite. But still, this is one of the very few chances that you will get at GCSE level to actually be creative. And to my mind at least, that was always more enjoyable – if *enjoyable* is the right word – than simply demonstrating that I had memorised loads of facts.

You'd be surprised how cheaply you can get hold of poetry
these days!

My Last Duchess
Robert Browning

FERRARA

That's my last Duchess painted on the wall,
Looking as if she were alive. I call
That piece a wonder, now; Fra Pandolf's hands
Worked busily a day, and there she stands.
Will't please you sit and look at her? I said
"Fra Pandolf" by design, for never read
Strangers like you that pictured countenance,
The depth and passion of its earnest glance,
But to myself they turned (since none puts by
The curtain I have drawn for you, but I)
And seemed as they would ask me, if they durst,
How such a glance came there; so, not the first
Are you to turn and ask thus. Sir, 'twas not
Her husband's presence only, called that spot
Of joy into the Duchess' cheek; perhaps

Fra Pandolf chanced to say, "Her mantle laps
Over my lady's wrist too much," or "Paint
Must never hope to reproduce the faint
Half-flush that dies along her throat." Such stuff
Was courtesy, she thought, and cause enough
For calling up that spot of joy. She had
A heart—how shall I say?— too soon made glad,
Too easily impressed; she liked whate'er
She looked on, and her looks went everywhere.
Sir, 'twas all one! My favour at her breast,
The dropping of the daylight in the West,
The bough of cherries some officious fool
Broke in the orchard for her, the white mule
She rode with round the terrace—all and each
Would draw from her alike the approving speech,
Or blush, at least. She thanked men—good! but thanked
Somehow—I know not how—as if she ranked
My gift of a nine-hundred-years-old name
With anybody's gift. Who'd stoop to blame
This sort of trifling? Even had you skill
In speech—which I have not—to make your will
Quite clear to such an one, and say, "Just this
Or that in you disgusts me; here you miss,
Or there exceed the mark"—and if she let
Herself be lessoned so, nor plainly set
Her wits to yours, forsooth, and made excuse—
E'en then would be some stooping; and I choose
Never to stoop. Oh, sir, she smiled, no doubt,
Whene'er I passed her; but who passed without
Much the same smile? This grew; I gave commands;
Then all smiles stopped together. There she stands
As if alive. Will't please you rise? We'll meet

The company below, then. I repeat,
The Count your master's known munificence
Is ample warrant that no just pretense
Of mine for dowry will be disallowed;
Though his fair daughter's self, as I avowed
At starting, is my object. Nay, we'll go
Together down, sir. Notice Neptune, though,
Taming a sea-horse, thought a rarity,
Which Claus of Innsbruck cast in bronze for me!

Compare the ways poets present ideas about power in 'My Last Duchess' and one other poem from 'Power and Conflict.'

Introduction

I have opted to invoke 'Checking Out Me History' by John Agard for this particular comparison, because both poems are about controlling narratives. My philosophy insofar as the introduction is concerned is that it ought to be doing two things. First, it should be scoring early AO3 points by placing the poems in context. Second, it should be giving a hint as to where your discussion is heading, since, by doing so, you are allowing the examiner to gain their bearings and thus ready themselves to award you AO1 marks.

"Although Browning's mid-nineteenth-century dramatic monologue and Agard's post-colonial, free-verse protest are greatly different in style, both share a fascination with the power derived from controlling and shaping narratives.[1] However, whereas Agard's piece pillories the imbalances wrought by the forces who have historically controlled narratives, Browning's piece is in fact written from the perspective of just such a powerful individual: it explores his attempts to control the narrative surrounding his ex-wife."

Theme/Paragraph One: Both poems explore how power is brokered by those in control of the narrative. In 'Checking Out Me History,' the narrator is self-consciously pointing this out, as he rails against the power of the dominant historical narrative. 'My Last Duchess,' however, is written from the perspective of the individual who is in fact in control of the narrative.

- In Agard's poem, there is an explicit awareness that power is brokered by those forces who decide which areas of history and culture are worthy of attention: his refrain 'Dem tell me' not only invokes the impersonal entity that arbitrates on the worthiness of certain narratives, but also, through its repetition, mimics the incessant repetition in which dominant narratives reverberate through culture. As Agard enumerates the topics deemed worthy by the powers-that-be – '1066;' 'Dick Whittington;' 'de Cow who jump over de moon' – he outlines in shorthand the contours of a version of Britain's history and culture that constitute a kind of canonical, legitimised history. [*AO1 for advancing the argument with a judiciously selected quote*].

- However, Agard observes that, by overlooking his Guyanese cultural heritage – the heritage of a former colony – the dominant culture enacts a colonial erasure. He states that it functions to 'Blind me to me own identity.' The spondee at the line's start, as well as the physical violence evoked by 'blind me,' reflect the narrator's indignation at this attempt to remove his people's history from sight.[2] [*AO2 for the close analysis of the language; AO3 for placing the poem in historical context*].

- *Pivot to a comparison*: Browning's poem, however, does not rail against those who control narratives; rather, it dramatises a powerful individual's attempts to control a narrative. The narrator controls not only what his interlocutors hear, but also what they *see*: he takes pride in the fact that nobody else 'puts by / The curtain' concealing the duchess's portrait.[3] The poem becomes a study in how powerful entities peddle their narrative. Particularly striking is the narrator's use of self-deprecating rhetoric. By claiming he lacks oratory skill ('which I have not,' he claims), the narrator seduces his interlocutors into dropping their guard, ironically revealing his oratory prowess. [*AO1 for advancing the argument with a judiciously selected quote*].

Theme/Paragraph Two: Hegemonic power is presented as something that can in fact be challenged.[4] In 'Checking Out Me History,' the colonial narrative is challenged through a powerful alternative narrative, which places emphasis on the experience of the oppressed and marginalised.

In 'My Last Duchess,' the narrator's description of the Duchess inadvertently offers a case study of female sexuality challenging patriarchal command.

- Agard's poem does not simply posit the dangers of a dominant, colonial narrative: it also explores the power of counter-narratives that place emphasis instead on the experiences of the oppressed and marginalised. At the end of each of the stanzas that enumerate "traditional" British culture, Agard pitches an alternative cultural touchstone that he believes ought to be given weight: 'Nanny de maroon;' 'de Caribs and de Arawaks too.' By concluding these non-italicised stanzas with these counter-narratives, Agard uses structure to enact a literal undermining of the dominant narrative. [*AO1 for advancing the argument with a judiciously selected quote; AO2 for discussing how structure shapes meaning*].

- However, Agard takes his counter-narrative a step further: he interpolates italicised stanzas that elaborate on the stories that underpin his cultural touchstones. For instance, he discusses 'Touissant:' a 'slave / with vision / lick back / Napoleon.' The phrase 'with vision' is a wordplay: it refers to both Touissant's revolutionary vision, but also the poet's vision of an alternative version of history. [*AO2 for the close analysis of the language*].

- *Pivot to comparison*: In 'My Last Duchess,' there is no such explicit assertion of a counter narrative by the oppressed party. However, the narrator's description of the Duchess inadvertently offers a case study of jealous patriarchal power rattled by natural female behaviour.[5] Although the narrator seeks to convince the interlocutor that his duchess is ungrateful – 'she ranked / My gift of a nine-hundred-years-old name / With anybody's gift' – it is clear the narrator is attempting to excuse his jealousy and paranoia. The only transgressions he can identify are 'approving speech[es]' or the occasional 'blush' the duchess directs towards other men. [*AO1 for advancing the argument with a judiciously selected quote*].

- As a result, there is a secret counter-narrative lurking between the lines – a narrative in which a petty tyrant attempts to police every aspect of a young woman's life – and which, once seen, challenges the contours of the dominant narrative. Browning's poem therefore suggests that there is power in holding a dominant narrative up to scrutiny.

Theme/Paragraph Three: While shaping narrative is posited as the central battleground in both poems, each piece also explores other means by which dominant powers can be challenged.

- Perhaps most striking in 'Checking Out Me History' is the poet's attempt to manipulate and alter the English language. The English language is, in many ways, the most potent symbol of colonialism: it was imposed on other cultures – even threatening to erase the tongues of those cultures: Agard's native Guyana, which was colonised by Britain from 1796 onwards, is an English-speaking country to this day. By colonising English with idiosyncrasies of his own Creole tongue – 'dem tell;' 'bout dat' – Agard is enacting a counterpunch: he is powerfully subverting English's grammar and spelling in a way that ironically reverses English's subversion of the colonies' languages. [*AO1 for advancing the argument with a judiciously selected quote; AO2 for discussing how structure shapes meaning*].

- Agard uses form to achieve a similar result: in alternate stanzas, he forces English into the confines of two-and-three-word-long lines that jar with hegemonic patterns of English speech. [*AO2 for discussing how form shapes meaning*].

- *Pivot to comparison*: Browning's poem, however, explores a different method of challenging language-based narratives: visual art. Although Browning's narrator might attempt to foist an interpretation onto Fran Pandolf's 'design,' the mere presence of the artwork offers an alternative narrative. Of course, the potency of the painting to challenge the narrative is limited from a readerly point of view: we are unable to view the artwork. However, within the fictional universe conjured by the monologue, the interlocutors are able to see the 'Duchess painted on the wall' and will be deciding whether it tallies with the narrator's narrative, or in fact undermines it. [*AO1 for advancing the argument with a judiciously selected quote*].

Conclusion

There is no set way to tackle the conclusion. Sometimes I'll have an extra mini theme up my sleeve, and in that case I'll integrate it into the conclusion to satisfy AO1 criteria. It can also be a good opportunity to score some extra AO3 (historical context) marks, as I have done here. I suppose the key thing, as you are wrapping things up, is to ensure you keep one eye on the assessment objectives.

"Agard and Browning are both fascinated with the power of narrative, and how it allows those who control it to curate and delineate which historical events are deemed worthy of attention. However, Agard's piece more aggressively embraces the power of the counter-narrative. The poem is an attempt to pull back the 'curtain' that British colonialism has for so long drawn over his culture; to change the calls of 'notice Neptune,' as Browning's narrator exclaims at the poem's end, into notice 'Mary Seacole.'"

A vista from Agard's native Guyana

The Charge of the Light Brigade
Alfred, Lord Tennyson

I
Half a league, half a league,
Half a league onward,
All in the valley of Death
Rode the six hundred.
"Forward, the Light Brigade!
Charge for the guns!" he said.
Into the valley of Death
Rode the six hundred.

II
"Forward, the Light Brigade!"
Was there a man dismayed?
Not though the soldier knew
Someone had blundered.
Theirs not to make reply,
Theirs not to reason why,

Theirs but to do and die.
Into the valley of Death
Rode the six hundred.

III
Cannon to right of them,
Cannon to left of them,
Cannon in front of them
Volleyed and thundered;
Stormed at with shot and shell,
Boldly they rode and well,
Into the jaws of Death,
Into the mouth of hell
Rode the six hundred.

IV
Flashed all their sabres bare,
Flashed as they turned in air
Sabring the gunners there,
Charging an army, while
All the world wondered.
Plunged in the battery-smoke
Right through the line they broke;
Cossack and Russian
Reeled from the sabre stroke
Shattered and sundered.
Then they rode back, but not
Not the six hundred.

V
Cannon to right of them,
Cannon to left of them,
Cannon behind them

Volleyed and thundered;
Stormed at with shot and shell,
While horse and hero fell.
They that had fought so well
Came through the jaws of Death,
Back from the mouth of hell,
All that was left of them,
Left of six hundred.

VI
When can their glory fade?
O the wild charge they made!
All the world wondered.
Honour the charge they made!
Honour the Light Brigade,
Noble six hundred!

Compare the ways poets present ideas about conflict in 'Charge of the Light Brigade' and in one other poem from 'Power and Conflict.'

Introduction

On this occasion, I've decided to bring in Ted Hughes's 'Bayonet Charge,' perhaps my favourite poem in the collection. Again, notice how I start by quickly scoring AO3 marks for context, then start hinting at the thematic gist of my essay in order to pick up early AO1 marks.

"Tennyson's 'Charge of the Light Brigade' and Hughes's 'Bayonet Charge' centre on conflicts in which neither poet participated: the former, the nineteenth century Crimean War; the latter, WW2. Indeed, this is tacitly acknowledged through the removed third person perspective deployed in both poems. Yet despite this striking similarity, the pieces differ greatly in how they conceive of the patriotism that catalyses conflict, the role of the individual in war, and how they depict the horrors of battle."

Theme/Paragraph One: Whereas Tennyson sentimentalises the patriotism that seeks to justify the conflict, Hughes is scathing of these jingoistic forces.

- 'Charge of the Light Brigade,' by lionising obedient British soldiers who were slaughtered *en masse* as a result of a miscommunication, functions as propaganda in favour of fidelity to the national cause.[1] The fact the soldiers obediently died for their country renders them in the eyes of the poet 'hero[es]' whose glory is everlasting: 'When can their glory fade?' By situating this rhetorical question at the start of the sixth and final stanza, in an ode explicitly glorifying the 'the six hundred' who made the charge, the poet places structural emphasis on the glory he deems the soldiers to have earned through their patriotism. [*AO1 for advancing the argument with a judiciously selected quote; AO2 for the close analysis of the language*].
- Interestingly, Tennyson hints at the illogical

behaviour induced by this patriotism: he notes that, despite the soldiers' understanding that 'someone had blundered,' they still unquestioningly followed suicidal orders ('theirs but to do and die'). However, this acknowledgement is not followed by denouncement of patriotism's ills; instead, the reader is bombarded from all angles – 'to the right of them / ...to the left' – by a positive construal of the soldiers' obedience that tacitly reaffirms patriotic loyalty. [*AO1 for advancing the argument with a judiciously selected quote*].

- *Pivot to comparison*: Hughes's poem, however, is a far more withering take on patriotism: the 'patriotic tear' that had 'brimmed' in his soldier's eye – that is, the patriotism that had seduced him into fighting – has transmuted into something toxic: it is now 'sweating like molten iron from the centre of his chest.'[2] The patriotism is surreally rendered as a corrosive 'molten iron,' destroying him from within; and the trochaic words ('sweating,' 'molten') emphasise its unnaturalness. Indeed, patriotism – through the synecdochal stand-in of the King – is revealed in the heat of battle to be a mere triviality that can be dispensed of: 'King, honour, human dignity, etcetera / Dropped like luxuries.'[3] [*AO2 for the close analysis of the language*].

Theme/Paragraph Two: Whereas Tennyson conceives of war as something undertaken by a group, Hughes takes time to focus on the role of the individual while conflict is underway.

- Tennyson's poem relentlessly conceives of conflict as

conducted by groups as opposed to individuals. He repeatedly invokes the monolithic entity of 'the six hundred,' and the survivors, too, are only referenced as a group: 'All that was left of them / Left of six hundred.' Arguably, this group mentality is reaffirmed by the *mise-en-page*: the stanzas are labelled with Roman numerals, thereby using form to indicate that each is part of a larger group, and cannot be disentangled from said group.[4] [*AO1 for advancing the argument with a judiciously selected quote; AO2 for discussing how structure shapes meaning*].

- Interestingly, we do get snippets of reported speech, such as 'Forward, the Light Brigade,' which implicitly suggest the existence of individuals. However, not only is this undermined by the lack of attribution, but the speech itself refers to the soldiers as a group – namely, 'the Light Brigade.' [*AO2 for the close analysis of the language*].

- *Pivot to comparison*: Hughes, conversely, focuses on an individual: only one soldier appears on stage – the individual 'running.../ In raw-seamed hot Khaki.' This poem was written in the wake of two world wars with unprecedented casualties; as a result, Hughes's insistence of focusing on a single soldier may be understood as a reaction to violence that seemed to reduce individuals to statistics, and thus re-establish our ability to empathise. [*AO1 for advancing the argument with a judiciously selected quote; AO3 for placing the poem in historical context*].

- In an extended metaphor that renders the warring nations and the universe itself as the 'clockwork' of 'stars and...nations,' Hughes seems to almost cast this nameless soldier as the all-important second hand in the clock mechanism: 'Was he the hand pointing that second?' The metaphor both empowers and disempowers: on one hand, the lowly foot-soldier is the focal point; on the other, he is a powerless piece of apparatus in a larger mechanism. [*AO2 for the close analysis of the language*].

Theme/Paragraph Three: Another key discrepancy between the poems revolves around their portrayal of suffering as a result of conflict: whereas 'Bayonet Charge' delves unflinchingly into war's physical traumas, 'Light Brigade' sanitises violence.

- This difference is most clearly seen in their respective dealings with animals: whereas, in Tennyson's poem, the horse's death is dealt with glibly – 'While horse and hero fell' – in Hughes's, the reader is presented with a prolonged, disturbing image of a 'yellow hare,' presumably on fire, 'that rolled like a flame / And crawled in a threshing circle, its mouth wide / Open.' Not only does the sheer length of the description force the reader to consider the animal's pain, but the imagery – 'mouth wide / Open' – has the animal mimic a human expression of agony. [*AO2 for the close analysis of the language*].
- However, the poems also differ in how they broach human suffering. The reader is informed in Tennyson's poem that the soldiers 'Came through the Jaws of Death / Back from the mouth of hell;' yet while 'Death' and 'hell' *do* imply unpleasantness, this unpleasantness is never expanded on, and thus feels

abstract and unreal. Conversely, physical pain pervades Hughes's piece: even when the poet is describing inanimate objects such as the soldier's gun, the simile employed forces the reader to picture a maimed limb: 'Lugged a rifle numb as a smashed arm.' [*AO2 for the close analysis of the language*].

Conclusion

To wrap things up, I am going to invoke a third poem – one that is in fact not included in the anthology – to demonstrate contextual knowledge beyond merely commenting on historical circumstances (and thus score some bonus AO3 marks). I shall then use it as a means to tie up my argument...

"In Geoffrey Hill's 'September Song' (1968), Hill's narrator is the victim of the Nazi holocaust, even though Hill was not himself a victim: Hill uses this mode to force the reader to fully empathise with victims, to ensure they are not simply reduced to statistics. Hughes's poem deals with conflict in a similar way: it memorialises in a way that invites empathy. Tennyson's poem, however, stands in stark contrast: it seeks to sanitise war for political purposes; to glorify the act of sacrifice for one's country."

ESSAY PLAN THREE

'OZYMANDIAS' & 'KAMIKAZE'

Ozymandias
Percy Bysshe Shelley

I met a traveller from an antique land,
Who said—"Two vast and trunkless legs of stone
Stand in the desert. . . . Near them, on the sand,
Half sunk a shattered visage lies, whose frown,
And wrinkled lip, and sneer of cold command,
Tell that its sculptor well those passions read
Which yet survive, stamped on these lifeless things,
The hand that mocked them, and the heart that fed;
And on the pedestal, these words appear:
My name is Ozymandias, King of Kings;
Look on my Works, ye Mighty, and despair!
Nothing beside remains. Round the decay
Of that colossal Wreck, boundless and bare
The lone and level sands stretch far away."

Compare the ways poets present ideas

about power in 'Ozymandias' and in one other poem from 'Power and Conflict.'

For this essay, I have decided to compare Shelley's 'Ozymandias' to Beatrice Garland's 'Kamikaze.' Since they were written at very different points in time, I will start the essay by placing both pieces in context – and, in the process, will score early AO3 marks. I shall then signpost where my thematic argument is headed, so the examiner can start seeing where I'm planning to pick up my AO1 marks.

"Whereas Shelley's 'Ozymandias,' written in the wake of the French Revolution, seems suffused with the Romantic conceit that the artist might credibly challenge raw political power, Garland's post-WW2 piece, 'Kamikaze,' is more modest in scope, focusing on the implications of an isolated act of dissent.[1] However, despite these differences, they share common ground not only in their preoccupation with political power, but also in their fascination with the potency of storytelling and nature as potential brakes on political power."

Theme/Paragraph One: Ozymandias explores how political power is intrinsically temporal, whereas Kamikaze looks at how the cultural expectations that political power can spawn can persist from generation to generation.

- Shelley's central interest in 'Ozymandias' is the transience of political power: Ozymandias, the self-proclaimed 'King of Kings,' has been subverted by the relentless march of time. The description of the statue's likeness – relayed to the narrator by the traveller – insinuates that Ozymandias wielded considerable political power: its 'wrinkled lip, and sneer of cold command' is described as accurately capturing Ozymandias's power: 'its sculptor well those passions read.' The speech assigned to Ozymandias by the inscription – 'Look on my Works, ye Mighty, and despair!' – further emphasises the power he wielded: not only does the line start with two consecutive spondees, the ictuses resounding as if to emulate a booming timbre, but the phrase 'ye Mighty' is reminiscent of 'the almighty.' Ozymandias's power was comparable to that of God. [*AO1 for advancing the argument with a judiciously selected quote; AO2 for the close analysis of the language*].

- However, although Ozymandias's power was formidable, time has depleted it utterly. In the first line, the traveller is described as being from 'an antique land:' the implication is that the King's power, and those physical things that connote it, are now mere 'antiques' and curios. [*AO2 for the close analysis of the language*].

- *Pivot to comparison*: On the other hand, 'Kamikaze' explores how political power – and the cultural expectations it enforces – persists from generation to generation, undiluted by time. The Japanese pilot was shunned for failing to complete his patriotic duty of dying in battle. However, while the poem tantalisingly suggests the children who 'chattered and laughed' are immune to the cultural imperative to shun, the poem's denouement – placed in the final stanza for structural emphasis – indicates the children, too, eventually internalise the long-standing political expectations: 'gradually we too learned... / to live as though / he had never returned.'[2] [*AO1 for advancing the argument with a judiciously selected quote; AO2 for discussing how structure shapes meaning*].

Theme/Paragraph Two: Both poems present the power of storytelling – and of the artist in general – as a formidable force.

- In 'Ozymandias,' the traveller hints that, while Ozymandias might have had dominion over the sculptor, the sculptor was able to surreptitiously subvert the tyrant: the artist, as he 'stamped' Ozymandias's features into stone, subtly 'mocked them' with his 'hand.' The fact this subtly unflattering statue outlived the King is testament to the sculptor's power. [*AO1 for advancing the argument with a judiciously selected quote; AO2 for the close analysis of the language*].
- Yet the power of the artist is also explored through both the traveller and the poem's narrator: they are both artists – namely, storytellers – who, by communicating this description of the sculptor's unflattering work, further amplify the sculptor's power.
- *Pivot to comparison*: In 'Kamikaze,' the power of the storyteller is also evident: the poem's narrator tells the

story of the shunned pilot-cum-father, and, in so doing, induces a sympathy that undermines the political imperative to shun him.[3] The narrator lyrically relays the rich inner-monologue her father was likely experiencing *en route* to battle: she imagines that, as he looked at the sea, he 'remembered how he and his brothers [waited] on the shore' and 'built cairns of pearl-grey pebbles.' This description forces the reader to sympathise with the father – the 'pearl-grey pebbles' reminds us of the 'pearl-grey' matter between his ears that makes him uniquely human – and implicitly challenges the dehumanising ostracisation.[4] [*AO1 for advancing the argument with a judiciously selected quote*].

- However, although artists are portrayed as powerful in these poems, their weaponry is presented as flawed. In 'Ozymandias,' these artists, by working to subvert Ozymandias, ultimately assure the perpetuation of his legacy. In 'Kamikaze,' the storytelling ultimately proves incapable of preventing the next generation from shunning the pilot.

Theme/Paragraph Three: Ozymandias explores the brute power of nature and how it functions to level all men. On the other hand, nature in 'Kamikaze' has the power to inspire a love of life.

- If the power of the poet is a staple of Romantic poetry, so too is the power of nature, which is also present in Shelley's piece. Notably, it is not simply time that undercuts Ozymandias's power; it is nature itself. The traveller recounts how the statue is not only situated within an uncaring desert terrain – 'the lone and level sands stretch far away' – but have been rendered into 'colossal Wreck' through the process of 'decay.' The reader is left to infer that it is not simply time that had 'shattered' the statue's 'visage': it was also the processes of nature – the erosion wrought by the mighty desert – that took place during that time. [*AO1 for advancing the argument with a judiciously selected quote; AO3 for placing the text in a literary-historical context*].

- *Pivot to comparison*: However, whereas Shelley's desert possesses colossal destructive power, nature in Garland's poem is powerful insofar as it stokes the human imagination and engenders a love of life. In the narrator's telling, it is the moment that the pilot looks down 'on a green-blue translucent sea' – and those things adorning its natural tapestry – that he starts to second-guess his suicide mission.

- The way Garland places this phrase at the end of the second stanza, ensuring empty space beneath the words, not only has the form mirror the enormity of the sea's beauty, but also forces the reader to pause in much the same way as the pilot does. In 'Kamikaze,' the power of nature – with its 'green blue-sea' and 'dark shoals of fishes / flashing silver' – resides in its ability to inspire. [*AO2 for discussing how form shapes meaning*].

Conclusion

"Throughout Romantic literature, as it does in 'Ozymandias,' the idea that either art or nature might subvert political power appears time and again. Blake's 'Tyger' (1794) renders the eponymous animal – half artistic creation, half force of nature – as the epitome of political subversion.[5] However, while the aftermath of WW2 seemed to cast doubt on the ability of the artist to effect change, and indeed Garland's narrator-cum-artist is unable to end the shun, her poem does seems to suggest that nature has retained its ability to inspire political dissent."

The wreck of USS Arizona at Pearl Harbor. The Americans entered WW2 after the Japanese mounted this attack on a US Navy Base in 1941

ESSAY PLAN FOUR

'EXPOSURE' & THE PRELUDE

Exposure
Wilfred Owen

Our brains ache, in the merciless iced east winds that
    knive us . . .
Wearied we keep awake because the night is silent . . .
Low drooping flares confuse our memory of the
    salient . . .
Worried by silence, sentries whisper, curious, nervous,
But nothing happens.

Watching, we hear the mad gusts tugging on the wire,
Like twitching agonies of men among its brambles.
Northward, incessantly, the flickering gunnery
    rumbles,
Far off, like a dull rumour of some other war.
What are we doing here?

The poignant misery of dawn begins to grow . . .

We only know war lasts, rain soaks, and clouds sag
    stormy.
Dawn massing in the east her melancholy army
Attacks once more in ranks on shivering ranks of grey,
But nothing happens.

Sudden successive flights of bullets streak the silence.
Less deadly than the air that shudders black with snow,
With sidelong flowing flakes that flock, pause, and
    renew,
We watch them wandering up and down the wind's
    nonchalance,
But nothing happens.

Pale flakes with fingering stealth come feeling for our
    faces—
We cringe in holes, back on forgotten dreams, and stare,
    snow-dazed,
Deep into grassier ditches. So we drowse, sun-dozed,
Littered with blossoms trickling where the blackbird
    fusses.
—Is it that we are dying?

Slowly our ghosts drag home: glimpsing the sunk fires,
    glozed
With crusted dark-red jewels; crickets jingle there;
For hours the innocent mice rejoice: the house is theirs;
Shutters and doors, all closed: on us the doors are
    closed,—
We turn back to our dying.

Since we believe not otherwise can kind fires burn;
Now ever suns smile true on child, or field, or fruit.

For God's invincible spring our love is made afraid;
Therefore, not loath, we lie out here; therefore were
    born,
For love of God seems dying.

Tonight, this frost will fasten on this mud and us,
Shrivelling many hands, and puckering foreheads crisp.
The burying-party, picks and shovels in shaking
    grasp,
Pause over half-known faces. All their eyes are ice,
But nothing happens.

Compare the ways poets present the effects of nature in 'Exposure' and in one other poem from 'Power and Conflict.'

Introduction

Since the question is asking us to focus on nature, I've decided to compare Owen's 'Exposure' to the extract from Wordsworth's *The Prelude*. My introduction seeks to acknowledge the different circumstances under which the two poems were written – Owen's during WWI and Wordsworth's during the Romantic period. I then broach the themes I intend to cover:

"Whereas one might expect an extract from Wordsworth's autobiography to engage with nature – nature, after all, was a perennial obsession of the Romantic movement – the centrality of the theme is perhaps more unexpected in Owen's sombre WW1 poem, 'Exposure.' However, while the poets deal with nature differently, there are still definite parallels, be it in their mutual preoccupation with nature's sublime power, or their focus on nature's ability to transmute both the imagination and the human body."

Theme/Paragraph One: In both poems, nature is presented as possessing sublime power; however, whereas in Wordsworth's work it is nature's aesthetic that is sublime, Owen's poem focuses on nature's capacity to dole out sublime physical punishment.

- In Wordsworth's *The Prelude*, the 'craggy ridge' becomes a literal focal point, as the narrator observes that, as he set out rowing, he 'fixed his view / Upon the summit.' However, the most striking aspect of this 'craggy ridge' is the fact it seems to represent the end of the world itself: the narrator describes it as 'The horizon's utmost boundary.' The litany of disruptive, inverted trochaic feet here – 'utmost' 'boundary' – almost seems to mimic the way in which the 'ridge' not only disrupts the horizon, but also seems on the brink of exceeding its bounds altogether.[1] [*AO1 for advancing the argument with a judiciously selected quote; AO2 for the close analysis of the language*].
- However, as the narrative unfolds, this sublime aesthetic is only redoubled: from behind this 'craggy steep,' seemingly 'the horizon's bound,' another

natural structure – 'a huge peak, black and huge' – somehow appears beyond the limit's limit.

- *Pivot to comparison*: Yet while the focus in Wordworth's poem is on nature's sublime aesthetic – on a personified mountain that, as it 'upreared its head,' achieves an overwhelming visual tableau – Owen's poem explores a different type of sublime: nature's capacity to dole out transcendent physical punishment. However, Owen also leans on personification to communicate nature's whips and scorns: he invokes a 'Dawn' who masses a 'melancholy army' and an 'air' that 'shudders.'[2] Yet nature in Owen's poem ultimately draws its power from physicality as opposed to aesthetics: it leaves the men 'cring[ing] in holes.' [*AO1 for advancing the argument with a judiciously selected quote*].

Theme/Paragraph Two: Whereas, in *The Prelude*, nature stimulates the imagination, in 'Exposure,' nature is so physically punishing that retreating into the imagination becomes a coping mechanism for the soldiers.

- While the cliffs startle Wordsworth's poet-cum-narrator, they do not paralyse his imagination so much as set it galloping apace. Indeed, the very existence of this poem – whose continuous single-stanza form visually reflects the cliff that inspired it – appears to be testament to the impact of the natural world on the poet's imagination.
- However, there is also clear evidence within the poem that the cliffs impacted emphatically on the narrator's

imagination: at the poem's dénouement, he reflects on how: 'Huge and mighty forms / moved slowly through [his] mind.' The language creates a sense of lasting impression: they 'moved slowly,' refusing to budge. Yet most interesting is the idea that these 'forms' were 'a trouble to [the poet's] dreams.' In eighteenth century literature, dreams were intimately linked with imagination (Horace Walpole's *The Castle of Otranto* was a rendering of a dream), hammering home the idea that these natural 'forms' fed the imagination.[3] *[AO1 for advancing the argument with a judiciously selected quote; AO3 for invoking for placing the text in its literary context].*

- *Pivot to comparison*: Yet whereas nature is the locus of imagination in *The Prelude*, in 'Exposure' it arouses imagination in a vastly different way: the soldiers deploy imagination in reaction to the pain induced by nature, to escape its torments. The narrator poignantly notes how 'slowly' their 'ghosts drag home' – their ghosts a symbol of their wandering minds – and conjure up comforting images: 'sunk fires, glozed / With crusted dark-red jewels,' the enjambment reflecting the smooth trajectory of the unshackled mind. However, this stanza packs a structural punch, finishing with a comment on imagination's limit in the face of raw nature: 'We turn back to our dying.' *[AO1 for advancing the argument with a judiciously selected quote; AO2 for the close analysis of the language and for discussing how structure shapes meaning].*

Theme/Paragraph Three: While in *The Prelude* nature functions to galvanise the poet-cum-

narrator physically, it does the reverse to the soldiers in 'Exposure,' reducing them to a state of utter stasis.

- In *The Prelude*, the poet's physical motion is a central focus: he describes 'stepping into' the boat; he narrates his rowing ('I rose upon the stroke'); and he recounts, too, the boats motion ('heaving through the water like a swan'). However, this motion is contingent on the natural world: not only does it take place in nature, but it is the sublime cliff that appears to be magnetically attracting the poet. Indeed, when the cliff later induces something akin to terror, it still galvanises motion, though this time it repels the narrator: 'With trembling oars I turned, / And through the silent water stole.' [*AO1 for advancing the argument with a judiciously selected quote*].
- But if Wordsworth's cliff is something that pulls and pushes the narrator, the snowstorm in Owen's piece is a phenomenon that renders the narrator and his fellow soldiers still. The soldiers are frequently described as motionless: the narrator at one point observes that 'we drowse' – the phrase 'drowse' evoking a state near unconsciousness; at another, that 'this frost will fasten on...us,' which insinuates the cold locks them in place. Indeed, even when they manage to muster energy to move and, with 'picks and shovels,' bury the dead, the anecdote finishes with the static image of the dead men's expressions: 'All their eyes are ice.' [*AO1 for advancing the argument with a judiciously selected quote; AO2 for the close analysis of the language*].
- This theme echoes through the poem with the refrain

'But nothing happens.' The use of *mise-en-page* – it always appears as an indented final line – emphasises the sense of stillness: the phrase appears to have been frozen in a fixed, immovable place. [*AO2 for discussing how form shapes meaning*].

Conclusion

Although, at this point, I feel confident that we have satisfied the exam board's criteria, I still have one final theme up my sleeve – namely, that in both poems, nature causes the narrator to contemplate the nature of God. So, since I have run out of space, I intended to include it in the conclusion:

"Both poems have at their centres an obsession with nature and the natural world: not only its power, but also its ability to move (or indeed freeze) us, both literally and figuratively. It might also be noted that in both poems nature even brings on theological contemplation. For Wordsworth's narrator, nature seems almost Godly (it takes forms 'that do not live / Like living men'), reflecting his pantheist worldview. For Owen's narrator, however, nature is so brutal that it seems to induce a deep scepticism of God's capacity for benevolence: 'love of God seems dying.'"

Scottish soldiers in a World War One trench

ESSAY PLAN FIVE

THE PRELUDE & 'STORM ON THE ISLAND'

Extract from *The Prelude*
William Wordsworth

One summer evening (led by her) I found
A little boat tied to a willow tree
Within a rocky cove, its usual home.
Straight I unloosed her chain, and stepping in
Pushed from the shore. It was an act of stealth
And troubled pleasure, nor without the voice
Of mountain-echoes did my boat move on;
Leaving behind her still, on either side,
Small circles glittering idly in the moon,
Until they melted all into one track
Of sparkling light. But now, like one who rows,
Proud of his skill, to reach a chosen point
With an unswerving line, I fixed my view
Upon the summit of a craggy ridge,
The horizon's utmost boundary; far above
Was nothing but the stars and the grey sky.
She was an elfin pinnace; lustily

I dipped my oars into the silent lake,
And, as I rose upon the stroke, my boat
Went heaving through the water like a swan;
When, from behind that craggy steep till then
The horizon's bound, a huge peak, black and huge,
As if with voluntary power instinct,
Upreared its head. I struck and struck again,
And growing still in stature the grim shape
Towered up between me and the stars, and still,
For so it seemed, with purpose of its own
And measured motion like a living thing,
Strode after me. With trembling oars I turned,
And through the silent water stole my way
Back to the covert of the willow tree;
There in her mooring-place I left my bark, –
And through the meadows homeward went, in grave
And serious mood; but after I had seen
That spectacle, for many days, my brain
Worked with a dim and undetermined sense
Of unknown modes of being; o'er my thoughts
There hung a darkness, call it solitude
Or blank desertion. No familiar shapes
Remained, no pleasant images of trees,
Of sea or sky, no colours of green fields;
But huge and mighty forms, that do not live
Like living men, moved slowly through the mind
By day, and were a trouble to my dreams.

**Compare the ways poets present nature in
The Prelude and in one other poem from
'Power and Conflict.'**

Introduction

In the previous essay, we looked at nature on Owen's 'Exposure' and Wordworth's *The Prelude*; however, there is another key nature poem in the collection – Seamus Heaney's 'Storm on the Island.' So, in order to illustrate the flexibility of the thematic method, I shall this time draw a comparison between *The Prelude* and 'Storm on the Island.'

> "Whereas Wordsworth's fascination with nature is to be expected – nature was a chief concern of the Romantic movement – Heaney's fascination is more at odds with his time of writing: his pastoral imagery seems almost as though a protest against the technologically advanced post-WW2 society in which he lives. However, while the poets conceive of nature in very different ways, there is an acknowledgement in both of the threat it can represent."

Theme/Paragraph One: In 'Storm on the Island,' humans appear to be passive, and nature seems to be actively seeking them out. In *The Prelude*, on the other hand, it is the poet that is actively seeking nature out; however, nature is not passive – it reacts by seemingly chasing the poet down.

- In Heaney's poem, nature is cast as the active entity that seeks out and attacks, whereas humans are cast as passive entities, hunkering down for a siege. The opening lines of the poem acknowledge the siege mentality of the narrator and his fellow islanders: they have 'prepared' for nature's onslaught by building 'squat' houses and 'sink[ing] walls in rock.' Nature is implicitly present in these lines, since it is the entity for which they are preparing. [*AO1 for advancing the argument with a judiciously selected quote*].

- Sure enough, once it makes an appearance in the form of the eponymous storm, Heaney personifies it to place focus on its agency: it is 'the thing you fear' – a kind of Grendelesque monster – that 'pummels your house' and 'strafes invisibly' and 'bombard[s].'[1] The diction 'strafes' and 'bombarded' are military, thereby casting nature as a hostile force, whereas the word 'pummels' implies brute force – its trochaic cadence reflecting how the wind knocks the environs off kilter. [*AO2 for the close analysis of the language*].

- *Pivot to comparison*: For Wordsworth, however, the human entity is not passive; the narrator/Wordsworth (it is an autobiographical poem) seeks out natural phenomena: he steals a boat ('I unloosed her chain') and ventures across 'the silent lake.' The littering of 'I' – 'I dipped my oars;' 'I rose upon my stroke' – places emphasis on the narrator's agency. [*AO2 for the close analysis of the language*].

- However, the natural world around him does not sit idly by. Instead, as Wordsworth progresses, 'the craggy steep' rises into view: 'as if with voluntary power instinct, / Upreared its head.' Just as in Heaney's piece, personification is used to draw attention to the natural landscape's agency. Moreover, the two inverted trochaic feet created by the words 'powers instinct' neatly reflects the shift in agency from the narrator to the 'steep.' [*AO2 for the close analysis of the language*].

Theme/Paragraph Two: In 'Storm on the Island,' Heaney seems fascinated by the absence and emptiness of nature. In contrast, Wordsworth, the pantheist, sees nature as so present, so full of objects of fascination, that he is unable to dislodge it from his mind.

- Although nature is at the heart of Heaney's poem, a large amount of focus is paradoxically on its emptiness and absence. The poem's *denouement* hones in explicitly on this nothingness: the narrator observes that the island is 'bombarded with the empty air,' and finally that 'it is a huge nothing that we fear.' On a literal note, the narrator is perhaps meditating on the fact that high winds are only visible insofar as they impact on other phenomena. However, in spite of his personification earlier in the poem, it could in fact be a meditation on the sheer lifelessness of the storm: it is not a living, breathing thing; the storm is the antithesis to life and substance. [*AO2 for the close analysis of the language*].

- The structural choice to end the poem with this assertion – a kind of closing 'salvo,' to borrow Heaney's diction – ensures that the reader is left with no choice but to confront nature's intrinsic emptiness. [*AO2 for discussing how structure shapes meaning*].

- *Pivot to comparison*: In contrast, Wordsworth's narrator doubles down on the personification and seems to insist on the multitudes that reside within nature. He explicitly deploys a simile to imbue the landscape with life – 'like a living thing' – and uses other epithets to imply an inner, spiritual life: it is an 'elfin pinnacle;' it has a 'purpose of its own.' [*AO2 for the close analysis of the language*].

- This notion that nature contains magnitudes – a kind of deeper life – coheres with Wordsworth's personal philosophy. Wordsworth was a pantheist who construed nature as a physical manifestation of God. This is made explicit in such poems as *Tintern Abbey*, in which Wordsworth points to 'something far more deeply interfused' within the natural world. [*AO3 for placing the text in a literary-historical context*].

Theme/Paragraph Three: Both poems meditate on the capacity of the nature to inflict harm; however, whereas the harm Heaney focuses on is chiefly physical, the threat nature represents in the extract from *The Prelude* is far more psychological in nature.

- Heaney brings to mind the physical harm nature can bring about not only by using the military diction alluded to earlier, but also through rhetorical devices: in a particularly striking simile, he describes the storm-whipped ocean as spitting 'like a tame cat / Turned savage.' The poet, by placing a line break mid-sentence, uses form here to create suspense, but also enacts a violence to the line that mirrors the violence done to the island. [*AO1 for advancing the argument with a judiciously selected quote; AO2 for the close analysis of the language and for discussing how form shapes meaning*].
- *Pivot to comparison*: However, while the violence nature brings about in Heaney's poem is physical, the

trauma it inflicts in Wordsworth's piece is far more psychological. At the poem's climax, the image of the mountains haunts the narrator's thoughts. He talks 'Of unknown modes of being' that 'hung a darkness' over his thoughts: the word 'darkness' implying an inner turmoil. Indeed, the psychological impact of these 'mighty forms' is deeply reminiscent of Edmund Burke's concept of the sublime: a force that is both beautiful yet destructive.[2] [*AO2 for the close analysis of the language; AO3 for placing the text in a literary context*].

- Wordsworth continues to meditate on the psychological trauma right up until the final line, in which he discloses that they 'were a trouble to [his] dreams.' The trochaic word 'trouble' is broken over two iambic feet, thereby creating rhythmical tension that mimics the tension in the poet's mind. Moreover, the structural choice to place this confession of insomnia in the final line adds emphasis: the reader's final thoughts are with the psychological trauma nature inflicts. [*AO2 for the close analysis of the language and for discussing how structure shapes meaning*].

Conclusion

"Although written in vastly different eras, these poems share plenty of common ground in their perception of nature: both construe it as capable of doing harm, and both construe it as an active force. However, whereas Wordsworth sees divinity in nature, Heaney sees the storm as the embodiment of nothingness."

The Peak District, the slice of England where William
Wordsworth grew up

ESSAY PLAN SIX

'LONDON' & 'REMAINS'

London
William Blake

I wander thro' each charter'd street,
Near where the charter'd Thames does flow.
And mark in every face I meet
Marks of weakness, marks of woe.

In every cry of every Man,
In every Infants cry of fear,
In every voice: in every ban,
The mind-forg'd manacles I hear

How the Chimney-sweepers cry
Every blackning Church appalls,
And the hapless Soldiers sigh
Runs in blood down Palace walls

But most thro' midnight streets I hear
How the youthful Harlots curse

Blasts the new-born Infants tear
And blights with plagues the Marriage hearse

Compare the ways poets explore suffering in 'London' and in one other poem from 'Power and Conflict.'

Introduction

On this occasion, I decided to invoke Simon Armitage's 'Remains,' since it deals movingly with the suffering of PTSD sufferers.

"Although Blake and Armitage's poems deal with vastly different circumstances – the former with an eighteenth century London in which wealth inequality was rife; the latter with a kind of uniquely post-WW2 asymmetric warzone – both first-person narratives have at their heart the idea of human suffering. However, whereas both chart how suffering begets suffering, Blake's poem forces the reader to confront how this unfolds on a broader societal level."

Theme/Paragraph One: In both Armitage's 'Remains' and Blake's 'London,' the way the narrator travels through a geographical space helps them broach their feelings towards conflict and suffering.

- In Armitage's poem, the narrator, after killing the looter, is forced to walk through the scene of the murder: 'His blood-shadow stays on the street, and out on patrol / I walk right over it week after week.' As the narrator moves through the terrain on foot, he is forced to confront the implications of his murder time and again. The phrase 'blood-shadow' is particularly interesting: in the same way a shadow follows an individual as they walk, the shadow of this slain man follows the soldier as he walks, forcing him to contemplate the suffering he has wrought. Moreover, while the word 'patrol' might usually evoke the idea of physical motion combined with protecting and safeguarding, its use here is perhaps an intentionally ironic comment by the narrator. During the course of his patrolling, he has come to understand that it is in fact him and his cohort – given the suffering they have induced – that require patrolling. [*AO1 for advancing the argument with a judiciously selected quote; AO2 for the close analysis of the language*].

- *Pivot to comparison*: In Blake's poem, the narrator's movement through a geographical space, London, similarly forces him to confront and grapple with suffering. Indeed, his observation that 'I wander thro' each chartered street,' and the aural closeness between the word 'wander' and wonder,' hints at the way that walking enables him to reflect.[1] Most significantly, it is through the process of walking that the narrator is able to observe in individuals – 'mark in every face I meet' – the 'marks of woe' and suffering that are so central to the poem. [*AO2 for the close analysis of the language*].

- When the narrator later observes that he moved 'thro'

midnight streets,' he is not only reaffirming the fact he
is in motion, but he is also – through his reference to
'midnight' – symbolically suggesting that walking
allows him to see a darker side of London that would
otherwise be concealed from view. [AO2 *for the close
analysis of the language*].

**Theme/Paragraph Two: Whereas in 'Remains' the
narrator to some degree attempts to disengage
himself from the suffering of the looter he encoun-
ters, Blake's narrator seeks to fully empathise
with the pain of those around him.**

- The sheer level of detail with which Armitage's
  narrator recounts the brutal act he carried out
  indicates how he has been forced to grapple with the
  looter's suffering – he describes how he watched
  'every round as it ripped through his life,' and how he
  could see the 'broad daylight on the other side.'
  However, despite this, it is also clear that the narrator
  has ruthlessly attempted to disengage himself from his
  victim's suffering. This is indicated not only in his
  clinical description of his (and his colleagues')
  dealings with his body – they toss 'his guts back into
  his body' – but in his refusal to identify the looter.
  [AO1 *for advancing the argument with a judiciously
  selected quote*; AO2 *for the close analysis of the
  language*].
- *Pivot to comparison*: However, while Blake similarly
  opts to anonymise the sufferers he chances upon (he
  talks of 'every man;' and 'every infant's cry,' but
  nobody is named), the sense is not that he is refusing

to empathise with their suffering, but rather that he is attempting to empathise with a ubiquitous suffering that transcends any one individual. Indeed, the scale of the suffering is communicated through the fact the narrator feels the need to resort to surreal images of 'cries' and 'sighs' – symbols of suffering children and soldiers respectively – transmuting into soot and 'blood' on 'Church' and 'Palace' walls. The suffering is too grand to express in conventional images. The *abab* rhyme scheme indicates that the child 'Chimney sweepers' and the 'Soldier' – demographics exploited by eighteenth century society – are intimately bound by their suffering. [*AO1 for advancing the argument with a judiciously selected quote; AO2 for the close analysis of the language*].

- The narrators' differing mindsets tallies with the circumstances at play. Whereas the narrator is directly culpable for the looter's suffering in 'Remains,' and is thus struggling with the guilt, the suffering in 'London' is the result of broader societal ills, brought about by such entities as organised religion and an abusive monarchy (represented synecdochically by the 'Church' and 'Palace'). [*AO3 for placing the text in historical context*].

Theme/Paragraph Three: Both poems explore how suffering begets further suffering. In 'Remains,' the suffering inflicted on the looter leads to the narrator enduring terrible psychological trauma. In 'London,' the focus is on how suffering is handed down from generation to generation.

- In Armitage's poem, the narrator does not simply explore the immediate physical suffering of the looter; he also explores the psychological suffering he personally endures as a result of the experience. When the soldier returns home, he remains haunted by the murder: he talks about how, when he 'blink[s],' the looter 'bursts again through the doors of the bank,' indicating how the event plays in his head. The fact it also recurs during his sleep – 'Dream, and he's torn apart by a dozen rounds' – shows that this process is involuntary: it is embedded deep in his unconscious mind ('dug in behind enemy lines,' as the war-metaphor minded narrator puts it). The psychological pain is inexhaustible: it is always 'here and now' for the narrator. [*AO1 for advancing the argument with a judiciously selected quote; AO2 for the close analysis of the language*].

- *Pivot to comparison*: Blake's poem also explores the continuation of pain and suffering into the future; however, whereas in Armitage's poem it is the narrator's psychological pain that is ongoing, in Blake's piece it is society's pain that persists, passing from one generation to the next. In the final stanza, the narrator talks about the suffering of a young prostitute: 'the youthful Harlot's curse.' The word 'curse' is a play on words: she is swearing, but she has also been 'curse[d]' by society's exploitations. More significant, however, is the fact that her curse is directed at 'the new-born Infant,' and causes it to cry ('tear'): this young woman – undoubtedly a victim of societal exploitation – is now passing on the suffering to a still younger generation. [*AO1 for advancing the argument with a judiciously selected quote; AO2 for the close analysis of the language].*

Conclusion

"A heightened sense of suffering has long been understood as a staple of the Romantic movement of which William Blake was a part: one is reminded of Percy Shelley's infamous poetic line: 'I fall upon the thorns of life! I bleed!' However, Armitage's piece seems to prove that no artistic movement has an embargo on suffering. Indeed, for all his narrator's attempts to distance himself emotionally and physically from his victim and the traumas of twenty first century warfare, the suffering – both his victim's and his owns – remains at all times intimately 'near to the knuckle.'"

ESSAY PLAN SEVEN

'REMAINS' & 'WAR PHOTOGRAPHER'

American soldiers at the Second Battle of Fallujah (2004), an offensive during the Iraq War. The British also fought in the Iraq war – and it is likely this conflict that Armitage's poem alludes to in 'Remains.' We have opted not to reproduce Armitage's poem in full: it is still in copyright and we wish to respect that fact.

Compare the ways poets present ideas

about conflict in 'Remains' and in one other poem from 'Power and Conflict.'

Introduction

This time, I've decided to mount a comparison between Simon Armitage's 'Remains' and Carol Ann Duffy's 'War Photographer.'

"Both 'War Photographer' and 'Remains' delve into a uniquely modern form of post-WW2 warfare, in which low-level proxy wars are waged in distant lands and sectarian violence rules the day. These poems not only take an unflinching look at the physical realities of warzone violence and how that violence is processed in the peaceful West, but also the significance of the often malignant memories that arise from conflict."

Theme/Paragraph One. Both poems place under the microscope the physical violence that results from warfare; however, while 'Remains' goes into close intimate details, 'War Photographer' takes a more oblique approach.

- Armitage's poem tackles the physicality of warfare's violence in intimate detail: the shooting of the 'looter' by the narrator and his colleagues is relayed with cinematic precision – the narrator observes that, after unleashing bullets, he is able to 'see broad daylight on the other side' of the corpse, and that the corpse then came to rest 'sort of inside out.' The metre undoubtedly adds emphasis: the phrase 'I see broad daylight' starts the line with a pair of spondees, the ictuses resounding on the ear like gunshots.[1] However, arguably it is the deadpan, matter-of-fact tone – which is in itself an inversion of the sobriety one would expect (our expectations have been turned 'inside out') – that most deepens the horror. [*AO1 for advancing the argument with a judiciously selected quote; AO2 for the close analysis of the language*].

- *Pivot to comparison*: Not to be outdone, however, 'War Photographer' also delves into warzone violence: in the penultimate stanza, the photographer reflects on an incident in which someone is seemingly undertaking a mercy killing: 'how he sought approval / without words to do what someone must.' Although the violence is far less graphic than in 'Remains,' the ambiguity and obliquity in which the violence is approached arguably has a more haunting effect: the reader is not informed of the execution's logistics in these flowing, enjambing lines, yet is left with an image of the aftermath: 'the blood stained into foreign dust.' [*AO1 for advancing the argument with a judiciously selected quote; AO2 for the close analysis of the language*].

- However, a key difference between the poems is in how this violence is met. In 'Remains,' there is no mention of sympathy for the victim or the traumatized soldier, whereas in 'War Photographer' the readers of 'Sunday's supplement' at least grant some cursory sympathy: their 'eyeballs prick / with tears.'

Theme Paragraph Two: Both poems explore the

**seeming geographical remoteness of hot conflicts
– especially the degree to which they are construed
as such by Western civilisation.**

- These poems also deal with a sense of the
  geographical remoteness of hot conflicts. In 'War
  Photographer,' the locations hosting violence –
  'Belfast. Beirut. Phnom Penh' – stand in stark contrast
  to the darkroom's calm, ordered solitude, in which the
  photographer is 'alone' with his apparatus 'set out in
  ordered rows.' Although there is an irony that 'Belfast'
  is in fact close to England, there is a sense throughout
  the poem that the ground itself – or 'foreign dust' – in
  these warzones is fundamentally different: the poem
  notes how in 'Rural England,' it is inconceivable that
  'fields' might 'explode beneath the feet / of running
  children.' The line-break after 'feet' is particularly
  effective, mimicking the way in which the ground
  gives way. [*AO1 for advancing the argument with a
  judiciously selected quote; AO2 for discussing how
  form shapes meaning*].
- *Pivot to comparison*: The narrator in 'Remains' also
  conjures a sense of geographical remoteness: he
  describes the warzone as 'some distant, sun-stunned,
  sand-smothered land.' This alliterative description
  seems to evoke a Middle Eastern conflict – like the
  Iraq wars that punctuated the end of the twentieth
  century and the start of the twenty first. However,
  what is interesting in 'Remains' is the sense that
  trauma is able to transcend physical distance: when
  the soldier is 'home on leave' and reflecting on the
  events that transpired on this 'desert sand,' he is
  seemingly transported back with a mere 'blink.' [*AO2*

for the close analysis of the language; AO3 for invoking relevant historical context].

Theme/Paragraph Three: In both poems, memories are inextricably intertwined with conflict.

- In 'Remains,' memories of violence not only transcend distance, but also traumatise the PTSD-riddled narrator. The violence he doled out might have been physical, but the memories of them have 'torn apart' his mind. The way the narrator uses the word 'Sleep' and 'Dream,' followed by a comma, to start sentences for two consecutive lines in the sixth stanza communicates the point through form: the abruptness of these words mimics the abruptness of these unwanted memories. [*AO2 for discussing how form shapes meaning*].

- *Pivot to comparison*: Yet whereas the memories in 'Remains' are unsolicited, the photographer in Duffy's poem is – through the act of developing photos – intentionally resurrecting memories. The photographer also appears to be traumatised by memories, albeit to a lesser extent: his hands 'tremble.' However, the importance of these photos (and thus memories) in 'War Photographer' is their ability to memorialise. The war photographer construes memorialising conflict as a religious, moral duty: the darkroom is likened to 'a church,' the photographer to a priest 'intoning mass,' and the phrase 'All flesh is grass' – positioned at the stanza's end for structural emphasis – has an almost pseudo-biblical quality. [*AO1 for advancing the argument with a judiciously selected quote; AO2 for the close analysis of the language and for discussing how structure shapes meaning*].

Conclusion

"Duffy and Armitage make a considerable effort to capture the modern age's unique form of conflict, in which nuclear weapons have rendered nation-state conflicts a rarity. Both poets powerfully capture the interchangeability of the small-scale, messy conflicts that have taken their place: 'Belfast' blurs into 'Beirut,' the whole sordid business taking place in some anonymous 'distant... land.'"

ESSAY PLAN EIGHT

'TISSUE' & 'THE ÉMIGRÉE'

The Koran is the holy book in the Muslim religion and is referenced by Dharker in 'Tissue.' We have opted not to reproduce Dharker's poem in full: it is still in copyright and we wish to respect that fact.

Compare the ways poets present ideas

about power in 'Tissue' and in one other
poem from 'Power and Conflict.'

Introduction

Here I have decided to tackle two poems we have not yet
broached: Imtiaz Dharker's 'Tissue' and Carol Rumens's 'The
Émigrée.'

"Both 'Tissue' and 'The Émigrée' – poems written in a
post-WW2 environment, in which a preference for
free verse predominates – seek to explore the persistent
power of language and imagination in an increasingly
dislocated world. However, whereas Dharker's poem
explores these concepts in an abstracted way, Rubens's
piece pits language and imagination against the brute
force of an oppressive machinery that has subjugated
the city from which she hails."

**Theme/Paragraph One: Power is brokered
through language – as well as the materials on
which language appears – in both poems. In 'Tissue,' it can plan the buildings in which we live,
delineate our identities, and keep a record of our
histories. In 'The Émigrée,' the power of language
is explored through an oppressive state that
considers language a threat.**

- In 'Tissue,' there is a prevailing sense that power is
  brokered not only through language, but also the

'paper' on which it appears. Early on, Dharker invokes the back pages of 'the Koran' in which 'a hand / has written in the names and histories.' The overwhelming impression is not just that these written-on pages have been cherished – the paper has been caressed so much that it has 'turned / transparent with attention' – but also that, by inscribing this information on paper, the people to whom it refers have been granted a powerful immortality on par with a holy book itself. [*AO1 for advancing the argument with a judiciously selected quote*].

- However, Darker explores not only language's power to maintain a collective memory, but also to signify the concepts that run our lives – particularly our money, and therefore our relationships to each other. The receipts ('fine slips') we receive 'from grocery shops' (a symbol of our monetary system) control us to such a degree that human 'lives' are ironically what ought be considered the metaphorical 'paper kites,' whereas the literal paper, and the markings on it, are the metaphorical kite-flyers. [*AO2 for the close analysis of the language*].

- *Pivot to comparison*: A similar conceit is seen in Rumen's 'The Émigrés,' in which the narrator observes that she has 'no passport' and thus 'there's no way back.' She is tacitly acknowledging the power that a 'passport' – a document with specific inscriptions – has over her life. However, Rumens meditates even more directly on the power of language in the previous stanza. Her narrator explores how the forces occupying her childhood city have banned her indigenous language as a means of repression, thereby implicitly acknowledging its subversive power: 'it may by now be a lie, banned by the state.' Language's power is further acknowledged through the lyrical, transcendent way the narrator describes her 'child[hood]'s vocabulary:' she talks about 'every coloured molecule of it,' lending the aural experience of encountering the language a synesthesial visual quality. [*AO1 for advancing the argument with a judiciously selected quote; AO2 for the close analysis of the language*].

Theme/Paragraph Two: Both poems explore the power of illumination. In 'Tissue,' light – particularly sunlight – has the power to afford clarity to onlookers. In 'The Émigrée,' sunlight is a force that symbolically shields and protects the narrator's memories of the city as well as its indigenous language.

- In Dharker's 'Tissue,' although paper and language are significant tools for wielding power, their power is enhanced when coupled with illumination – which chiefly manifests in the poem in the form of sunlight. This is evidenced in the fifth stanza, in which the information-rich map seems to be given newfound clarity by the sun's illumination: 'the sun shines through / their borderlines, the marks.' The line break enhances the sense of revelation: the reader pauses, then is swiftly presented with the contents of the map. [*AO1 for advancing the argument with a judiciously selected quote; AO2 for discussing how form shapes meaning*].

- In basic terms, Dharker could be reflecting on the significance of light during the act of reading: without light, the reader would be quite literally left in the dark. However, light could also be construed in Dharker's poem as a symbol of something cleansing: she invites the light to enter the paper city in order to 'break / through... the shapes that pride can make.' The 'pride' is cleansed by the penetrative light.

- *Pivot to comparison*: If, for Dharker, light is able to enhance language's power, for Rumens, the two entities seem at times to almost be interchangeable. At the end of the second stanza she goes so far as to claim that her empowering childhood language 'tastes of sunlight.' However, for Rumens, light does not simply work to empower language; it also serves to empower her memory: in the second line, she describes her 'memory' of the city as 'sunlight-clear;' and even as she acknowledges that the city has since become 'sick with tyrants,' the sunlight-infused version of the city that exists in her memory still takes precedence: 'but I am branded by an impression of sunlight.' [*AO1 for advancing the argument with a judiciously selected quote; AO2 for the close analysis of the language*].

Theme/Paragraph Three: Both poems explore the power of the imagination to create surreal landscapes that transcend. In 'Tissue,' the reader is presented with a surreal image—of buildings made of paper, and, in so doing, creates a realm in which the poet is uniquely empowered. In 'The Émigrée,' the imagination is able to create a

surreal jaunt through the city as a way to protest the totalitarian oppression.

- In both texts, a key concern is the power of the poet's imagination and its ability to conjure surreal landscapes that offer a kind of transcendence. In 'Tissue,' the reader is presented with a surreal image of buildings made of paper: she notes how an 'architect' could substitute 'brick / or block' for paper, before imagining just such a cityscape: a 'grand design' that was 'never meant to last' and could 'fall away on a sigh.' By conjuring this visual image, Dharker is asserting the power of the imagination to conquer Newtonian physics; indeed, the *mise-en-page* – for example, the stanza break when she discusses 'brick / or block' – draws attention to the fact that her poem is a kind of structure, built out of paper and language. [*AO1 for advancing the argument with a judiciously selected quote; AO2 for the close analysis of the language and for discussing how form shapes meaning*].

- *Pivot to comparison*: Rumens uses a similar tactic in 'The Émigrée;' however, there is more at stake in this piece, since the power of imagination is going toe-to-toe with the dictatorship that has suffocated her childhood city. The final stanza, which sees the narrator go on a surreal jaunt through the city, while in the company of a personified embodiment of this same city ('my city takes me dancing through the city') is a saturnalian protest against the dictatorship that has taken her city hostage.[1] The ongoing conflict between her imagination's capacity to conjure surreal and powerful images, and the dictatorship, is captured in the final two lines: the hostile forces invade her dreamscape and 'mutter death,' while her imagination recruits 'sunlight' to fend them off. [*AO1 for advancing the argument with a judiciously selected quote; AO2 for the close analysis of the language*].

Conclusion

"Whereas in pre-1945 poetry, there was a notion that a poet had the power to transform the world, in the latter half of the twentieth century, this idea faded. However, these two poems in fact seem to swim against this popular tide with their striking affirmations of the transformative power of both language and the poet's imagination."

My Last Duchess
Robert Browning

FERRARA

That's my last Duchess painted on the wall,
Looking as if she were alive. I call
That piece a wonder, now; Fra Pandolf's hands
Worked busily a day, and there she stands.
Will't please you sit and look at her? I said
"Fra Pandolf" by design, for never read
Strangers like you that pictured countenance,
The depth and passion of its earnest glance,
But to myself they turned (since none puts by
The curtain I have drawn for you, but I)
And seemed as they would ask me, if they durst,
How such a glance came there; so, not the first
Are you to turn and ask thus. Sir, 'twas not
Her husband's presence only, called that spot
Of joy into the Duchess' cheek; perhaps

Fra Pandolf chanced to say, "Her mantle laps
Over my lady's wrist too much," or "Paint
Must never hope to reproduce the faint
Half-flush that dies along her throat." Such stuff
Was courtesy, she thought, and cause enough
For calling up that spot of joy. She had
A heart—how shall I say?— too soon made glad,
Too easily impressed; she liked whate'er
She looked on, and her looks went everywhere.
Sir, 'twas all one! My favour at her breast,
The dropping of the daylight in the West,
The bough of cherries some officious fool
Broke in the orchard for her, the white mule
She rode with round the terrace—all and each
Would draw from her alike the approving speech,
Or blush, at least. She thanked men—good! but
    thanked
Somehow—I know not how—as if she ranked
My gift of a nine-hundred-years-old name
With anybody's gift. Who'd stoop to blame
This sort of trifling? Even had you skill
In speech—which I have not—to make your will
Quite clear to such an one, and say, "Just this
Or that in you disgusts me; here you miss,
Or there exceed the mark"—and if she let
Herself be lessoned so, nor plainly set
Her wits to yours, forsooth, and made excuse—
E'en then would be some stooping; and I choose
Never to stoop. Oh, sir, she smiled, no doubt,
Whene'er I passed her; but who passed without
Much the same smile? This grew; I gave commands;
Then all smiles stopped together. There she stands
As if alive. Will't please you rise? We'll meet

The company below, then. I repeat,
The Count your master's known munificence
Is ample warrant that no just pretense
Of mine for dowry will be disallowed;
Though his fair daughter's self, as I avowed
At starting, is my object. Nay, we'll go
Together down, sir. Notice Neptune, though,
Taming a sea-horse, thought a rarity,
Which Claus of Innsbruck cast in bronze for me!

Compare the ways poets present memory in 'My Last Duchess' and in one other poem from 'Power and conflict.'

Introduction

For our final essay plan, I decided to take on Browning's 'My Last Duchess' for a second time, and, on this occasion, to compare it to Jane Weir's 'Poppies.'

"Although 'My Last Duchess' and 'Poppies' are products of vastly different eras – a nineteenth century fascinated with psychological Gothic and a twenty-first century coping with the traumas of asymmetric warfare respectively – both of these first-person narratives have at their hearts a primordial concern about memory. In both, the extent to which the reader is granted access to the past is dependent on the personality of the narrator; moreover, both tether memories to key objects (namely, a paper poppy in Weir's piece, and a portrait in Browning's)."

Theme/Paragraph One: The fidelity of memory is dependent on the reliability of the narrator. In 'Poppies,' the narrator's grief causes a distortion to memory. In 'My Last Duchess,' the narrator is unreliable, his psychopathic intentions warping the recounting of his memories.

- In 'Poppies,' while the narrator's memories are presented as potent, the ability of memories to carry the past into the present is compromised by the narrator's grief. The narrator's memory has captured and preserved her experience of pinning a poppy to her son's lapel 'Three days before Armistice Sunday.' Indeed, we are treated to precise minutia: the 'crimped petals;' 'spasms of paper red'; the 'blackthorns of...hair.' However, while the memory is potent, it is compromised by the narrator's grief, which leads to a confusing timeline: the reader is not told the year in which this Armistice Sunday occurred. The timeframe also becomes hazy in the third stanza, where the reader is suddenly shuttled forward in time to the narrator studying 'inscriptions on the war memorial' and apparently now mourning her son's death. [*AO1 for advancing the argument with a judiciously selected quote; AO2 for the close analysis of the language*].
- *Pivot to comparison*: In 'My Last Duchess,' the vividness with which the narrator relays his memories

of the Duchess implies that his mind has no issue retaining details. In fact, unlike Weir's narrator, the reader is given a firm sense of the timeline: when he recounts how he ordered her execution – 'I gave commands; / Then all smiles stopped together' – there is a clear sequence of events. [*AO1 for advancing the argument with a judiciously selected quote*].

- However, if Weir's narrator was unreliable due to her fraught emotional state, Browning's is unreliable due to psychopathic tendencies. While discussing how his Duchess spoke kindly to other men ('would draw from her... approving speech'), he also reveals his resentments: he begrudges that his Duchess had not been more fawning, given his aristocratic roots ('nine-hundred-years-old name'). As a result, the reader is left uncertain whether his account of the Duchess's transgressions have been distorted by vanity, insecurity, or self-delusion. [*AO1 for advancing the argument with a judiciously selected quote*].

Theme/Paragraph Two: In both poems, there are key objects that are bound to the narrator's memory of the deceased individual. In 'Poppies', the poppy is intimately linked to the narrator's memories of her son, but also links her memory to the wider collective memory of those lost at war. In 'My Last Duchess,' the painting is linked to the narrator's memory of the Duchess.

- In Weir's poem, the poppy she 'pinned...onto [her son's] lapel' is more than just an inanimate object. It is both a focal point that gives her memories shape, but also an object that links her memories of a lost loved one to the memories of others who have lost loved ones. It is striking that the mention of the 'crimped petals' appears in the fourth line of the first stanza – that is, the stanza's centre – which structurally bolsters the notion that the poppy is the focal point of the memory. However, while this poppy is the object around which her memory is organised, it also symbolically links her memories to those of others who might also find a family member's name on 'the inscriptions on the war memorial'; in other words, individuals who have also lost loved ones at war. The poppy links the narrator's memory to a pool of kindred memories. [*AO1 for advancing the argument with a judiciously selected quote; AO2 for discussing how structure shapes meaning*]

- *Pivot to comparison*: Browning's poem similarly features an object that functions to refresh memories, and provide a focal point for said memories – namely, Fra Pandolf's portrait of the 'Duchess painted on the wall.' When the narrator points to 'the depth of passion' in the painted 'Duchess's earnest glance,' it is clear that his memories are inextricably intertwined with the portrait, since it immediately induces him to invoke memories of others eliciting the same reaction.

- Indeed, one might note that the object also links the narrator's memories of the Duchess to Fra Pandolf's; after all, the portrait is a manifestation of how Pandolf perceived the Duchess at the time of his painting her. Again, the object at the heart of the poem links the narrator's memories to the memories of others.

Theme/Paragraph Three: **Both poems invoke cultural/societal memories that allow the reader to better understand the meaning of the pieces.**

- Both poems also illustrate the potency of a different kind of memory: the cultural and societal memories that underpin human civilisation. In Weir's poem, the narrator invokes the biblical story of Noah's arc: she talks of releasing a 'song bird from its cage' and describes how, later, 'a single dove flew from the pear tree.' In the story of Noah's arc, the arrival of the dove with an olive branch connoted regeneration after the cataclysmic flood. By integrating such similar imagery in her poem – she releases a bird and is approached by a dove from a tree – she is using a cultural memory to infuse her poem with meaning: she is likening her son's departure to a cataclysm, and her ability to finally mourn him to a regeneration. [*AO1 for advancing the argument with a judiciously selected quote; AO3 for placing the text in a literary context*].

- It is worth noting that the line, 'released a song bird from its cage,' is rendered in iambic tetrameter. This metre is a nod to the more regimented English verse that came before it, thus reminding the reader of the cultural memory on which it draws.[1] [*AO2 for close language analysis; AO3 for placing the text in a literary context*].

- *Pivot to comparison*: In like fashion, Browning's poem also draws on cultural memory to supplement its meaning. At the poem's close, the narrator turns his attention to another curio in his possession, and alliteratively invites his interlocutor to do the same: 'Notice Neptune... / Taming a sea-horse.' By having his narrator invoke Neptune, the sea-god from Greek myth, Browning uses a cultural memory to enhance the reader's understanding of the narrator: the narrator perceives himself as a god, 'taming' a woman who he treats as if an animal: 'a sea-horse.' [*AO1 for advancing the argument with a judiciously selected quote; AO3 for placing the text in a literary context*].

Conclusion

"Weir and Browning's pieces both centre on narrators dealing with intimate memories, and raise questions about unreliable narrators hobbling the reader's ability to trust memories set out before them. However, the poet's use of cultural touchstones illustrates how shared cultural memory is an ever-powerful tool for imparting and shaping meaning."

In 2014, the Tower of London's moat was filled with 888,246 ceramic poppies. This artistic installation was put in place to mark one hundred years since the outbreak of the First World War

NOTES

ESSAY PLAN ONE

1. A dramatic monologue is used to describe a poem in which a narrator is giving a speech and, in the process, reveals aspects of his/her personality.

   Free verse refers to a type of poem that is not characterised by a regular rhyme scheme or a regular metre. It became increasingly popular post 1945.

2. I suspect you are probably asking: *what in the heck is a spondee?* Let me start from the top.

   GCSE students have often heard of the phrase iambic pentameter when talking about Shakespeare. The first word – iamb – refers to something called a metrical foot, whereas the word 'pentameter' refers to the fact that almost all of Shakespeare's lines have five metrical feet per line.

   It is almost certainly easiest to illustrate this with an example. Let's take the second line from Shakespeare's Romeo and Juliet; however, we are going to mark out each metrical foot with a vertical line, and all of the stressed syllables with bold font: 'In **fair** | Ve**ro**| na, **where** | we **lay** | our **scene.**' As you can see, each metrical foot here is made up of two consecutive syllables, making five metrical feet in all – hence pentameter (as opposed to, say, trimester, which would suggest that there are three feet). You can also see that the stress in each metrical foot is on the second syllable. This is what makes the metrical foot an iamb.

   So: *what is a spondee?* This is a type of metrical foot in which both syllables are stressed. Let's take a look at Agard's line, but let's mark out the feet and stressed syllables: '**Blind me** | to **me** | own i|**den**ti|**ty.**' Because Agard's poem – unlike Shakespeare's work - is rendered in free verse, there is no metrical regularity here. However, we can see that the first metrical foot has two stressed syllables, rendering it a spondee.

3. The interlocutor is the individual to whom a narrator is talking.

4. If something is hegemonic, it means it is dominant.

5. A patriarchal system is one in which men are the ones who hold the power. A system in which women are in charge is called the matriarchy.

ESSAY PLAN TWO

1. If you are lionising someone or something, it means you are glorifying it.

2. Transmute is another word for transform.

3. Synecdoche is when you use a part of something to refer to its totality. In

this instance, the poem refers to the King, but it is actually referring to the monarchy as a whole.

4. The *mise-en-page* refers to the way the text appears on the page.

ESSAY PLAN THREE

1. The French Revolution took place in 1789 and had a huge impact on Romantic poets.
2. Denouement is a French word that has entered into English usage and refers to the climax of a narrative.
3. 'Cum' in 'pilot-cum-father' is a Latin phrase. It basically means that the person in question is both of those things.
4. To ostracise someone is to exclude them from a wider group or society.
5. The word eponymous is used to describe a situation in which the title of a text is named after the main character.

ESSAY PLAN FOUR

1. In an earlier footnote, I explained that an iambic foot is a metrical foot in which the stress is on the second syllable. A trochaic foot, on the other hand, is when the stress is on the first syllable.

    But why have I called it an 'inverted trochaic foot?'

    The entirety of Wordsworth's 'The Prelude' is written in iambic pentameter (like Shakespeare's plays). So let's look at the opening line of the extract from 'The Prelude' that AQA have set, and use a vertical line and bolded font to mark out the metrical feet and the stressed syllables respectively: 'One **sum**|mer **eve** | ning (**led**| by **her**)| I **found**.' As we can see, we have five metrical feet (hence pentameter), all of which are iambs.

    Now, let's take a look at the line I was discussing in the essay plan above: 'The ho|**riz**on's | **ut**most | **bound**ary; | **far** a|**bove**.' As you can see, the second, third, fourth and fifth metrical feet all have the emphasis on the first syllable, thus making them trochees. We call them inverted because the vast majority of the poem is rendered in iambs – therefore, they are an inversion of the usual metrical pattern.

    You might also notice that the first metrical foot has no stresses whatsoever. This is known as a pyrrhic foot. You might notice, too, that there is one stray stressed syllable at the end of the line. This is known as a 'stressed hyperbeat' or a 'masculine ending.' Equally, if it had been unstressed, it would be described as an 'unstressed hyperbeat' or a 'feminine ending.'

2. As an aside, the phrase I've used here – namely, 'whips and scorns' – in fact comes from Shakespeare's *Hamlet*!

3. Horace Walpole's The Castle of Otranto is in fact considered the very first Gothic novel.

ESSAY PLAN FIVE

1. Grendel is a monster who appears in the Old English poem 'Beowulf.' The reason I've brought this up is because, in 1999, Seamus Heaney translated 'Beowulf' into modern English – and, indeed, it is famously a work of literature that he has held close to his heart.
2. Edmund Burke was an eighteenth century philosopher and politician.

ESSAY PLAN SIX

1. Aural refers to how things sound.

ESSAY PLAN SEVEN

1. An ictus is a word to describe a stressed syllable.

ESSAY PLAN EIGHT

1. The Saturnalia was a Roman festival that revolved around merriment and the reversal of roles. If something is saturnalian, it is characterised by qualities associated with this festival.

ESSAY PLAN NINE

1. Iambic tetrameter indicates that the line contains four iambic feet.